IT'S SCIENCE!

You and Your Body

Sally Hewitt

SCHOLASTIC INC.

New York Toronto London Auckland Sydney
Mexico City New Delhi Hong Kong Buenos Aires

Acknowledgments: Sally and Richard Greenhill p.15t; Robert Harding p. 15b (Warren Morgan); Image Bank p. 17t; Shout Picture Library p. 22br. All other photography commissioned by Franklin Watts. Thank to our models Candice Halliday, Connie Kirby, Jasmine Sharland, Charlotte Harrison, Zak Broscombe-Walker, Anton & Jamelle Allen, David Watts, Paul Hardcastle, Olivia Anysz, Lauren Shoota, Stephan Lee, Jordan Hardley, Camilla Knipe, James Moller, Charlie Lucas, Sumire Fujimoto and Ken King

Series editor: Rachel Cooke
Designer: Mo Choy
Picture research: Alex Young
Photography: Ray Moller unless otherwise acknowledged
Series consultant: Sally Nankivell-Aston

ISBN 0-516-23861-2

12 11 10 9 8 7 6 5 4 3 2 1   2 3 4 5 6 7/0

Printed in the U.S.A.

First Scholastic printing, February 2002

Contents

Name the Parts

Have a look at yourself in the mirror. Every part of your body that you can see has a name.

On this page we have named some of the parts of the body. What other parts can you name?

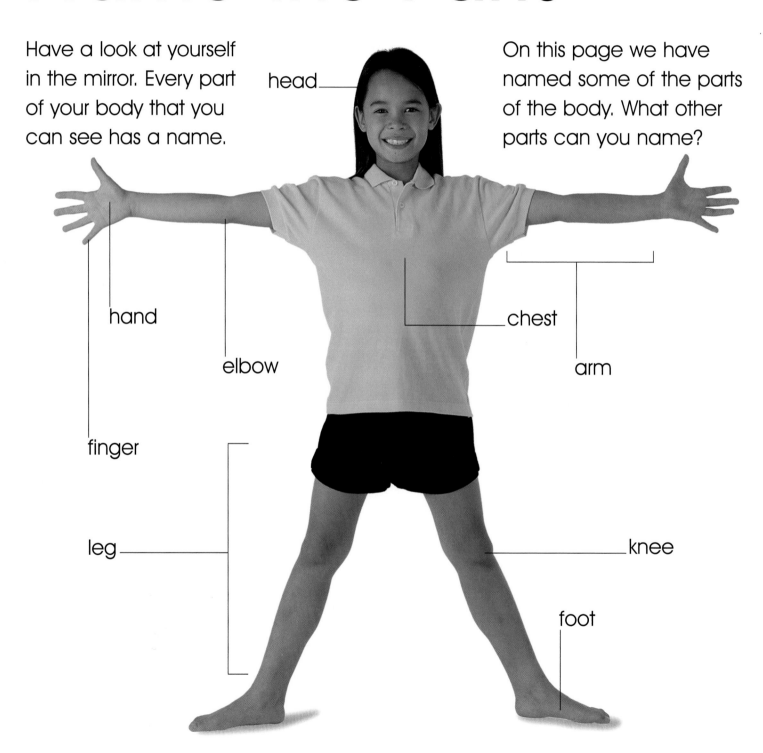

head

hand

elbow

finger

leg

chest

arm

knee

foot

Different parts of your body often work together.

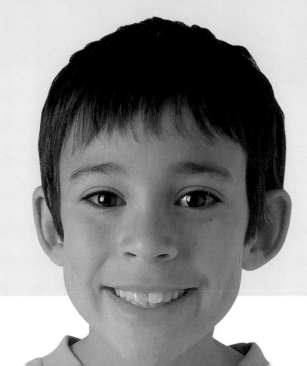

 TRY IT OUT!

Bend down and take off your shoe. You used your eyes to see your shoe and your hands to take it off. Which other parts of your body did you move and use?

Each part of your body is in the right place and is a good shape for the special job it does.

You use your hands for holding a pencil.

You walk, run, and jump on your feet.

How else do you use your hands and feet?

 THINK ABOUT IT!

Your eyes are in a good place for seeing. Imagine what it would be like if your eyes were in the back of your head!

7

You Are Special!

Lee, Martha, Abi, and Carl look different from each other. They all enjoy doing different things.

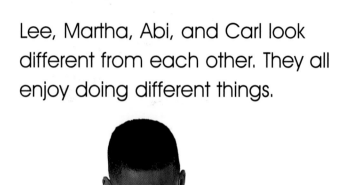

You are special, too. No one else in the world is exactly the same as you. What do you enjoy doing? What are you good at?

Everyone is different, but we all have lots of things that are the same. What things are the same about you, Lee, Martha, Abi, and Carl? How do your bodies work?

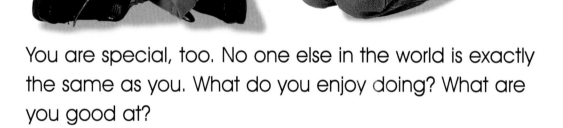

THINK ABOUT IT!

Usually you can recognize someone right away just by looking at them. People are different sizes. Hair, skin, and eyes can all be different colors. What else can be different about the way people look?

Voices are different, too. You might recognize someone's voice on the telephone.

TRY IT OUT!

Collect some facts about your friends like this. Do any friends have the same answers to all four questions? How similar are they in other ways?

	Color of hair	Color of eyes	Size of feet	Favorite food
Lee	brown	brown	12	ice cream
Martha				
Abi				
Carl				

Making Sense

How do you think Carrie knows that the apple is delicious, the teddy bear feels soft, and her t-shirt is yellow? She uses her **senses**.

Senses let you see, hear, smell, taste, and feel what is going on around you. You see with your eyes, hear with your ears, smell with your nose, taste with your tongue, and feel with your skin.

What else can Carrie find out about the things around her using her senses?

 **LOOK AGAIN**

Look again at page 9. What senses do you use to recognize people?

Your **brain** is inside your head. It makes sense of the world around you.

Nerves connect your brain to the rest of your body. They are like tiny telephone wires that take messages to your brain all the time about what you see, hear, smell, taste, and feel.

Sometimes important messages are sent to your brain to keep you safe.

If you pick up something too hot, like this drink, you put it down quickly. A warning message is sent from your fingers to your brain that the mug—and the drink—might burn you!

 THINK ABOUT IT!

A trash can sometimes smells bad. What is the smell telling you?

11

Eating and Drinking

A delicious smell from a plate of food makes you feel hungry!
You need food to give you **energy**, to keep warm,
to grow, and to stay healthy.

Food can be put into four groups:

fat

carbohydrates

protein

fruit and vegetables

You should eat some
food from each of these groups
to get the nutrients you need every
day. You need to drink plenty of
water, too.

THINK ABOUT IT!

Do you have food from each
of these groups every day?
Do you eat more food from
one group than another?

Think about what happens to your food next time you have something to eat.

First you chew it up into smaller bits—then you swallow it. The mashed-up food goes down into your **stomach**. There, juices make the food even smaller so that your body can take the good parts from it.

Your body gets rid of the parts of the food it cannot use when you go to the toilet.

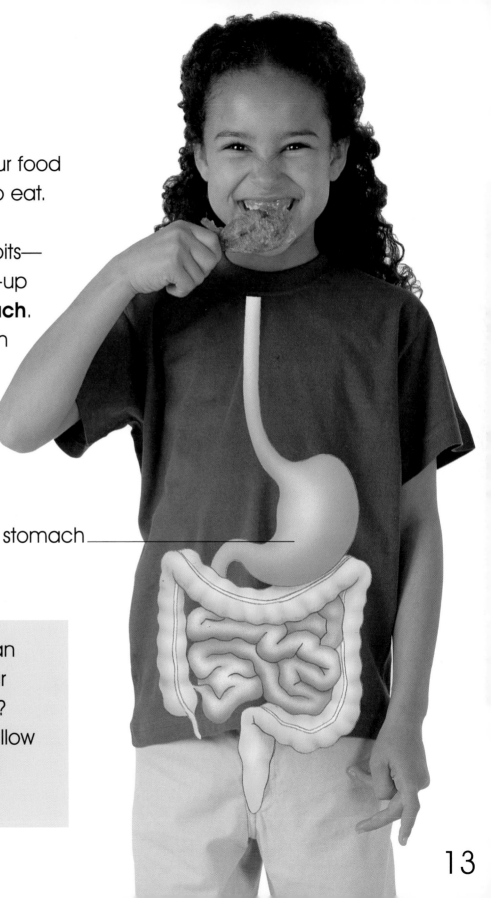

stomach_____

 **TRY IT OUT!**

Chew a mouthful of food. Can you feel slippery **saliva** in your mouth helping it to slip down? Feel your neck when you swallow —your food has started on its journey through your body.

Keeping Healthy

Usually, you feel fit and well. There are plenty of things you can do to stay that way. **Germs** can make you feel ill. They are too small to see, so you have to be careful not to catch them!

Germs stick to your hands, so always wash your hands before you eat. Germs in your stomach can make you feel sick.

Cold germs make you cough and sneeze. Use a handkerchief so no one else catches your germs!

 LOOK AGAIN

Look again at page twelve to find something else you can do to help you keep healthy.

14

Often when you feel ill, you soon get better if you rest. Sometimes you need medicine to help your body fight germs. You may go to the doctor for this medicine.

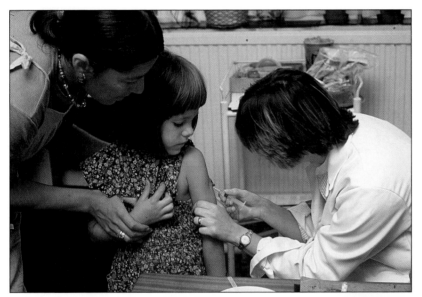

A doctor may give you an injection, too. An injection protects you from a **disease**, so it helps you stay healthy.

If you have an accident, you might have to go to the hospital. Hospitals give you special treatment, such as an operation or mending a broken arm.

 THINK ABOUT IT!

Have you ever been ill or had an accident? How did you feel? What did you do to get better?

15

Skin

Skin makes a very good covering for your body. It stretches when you move, it keeps out germs, it is waterproof, and it helps keep you warm in the cold and cool in the heat.

Melanin is a dark color in your skin that helps protect you from sunburn. The darker your skin, the more melanin you have.

☀ SAFETY WARNING!

Don't forget to wear a hat and use suntan lotion to protect you when you play in the sun.

Your skin is sensitive—you touch and feel things with it. The skin on your fingertips is very sensitive.
Blind people read with their fingertips. They use them to feel letters made up of little bumps.

Washing helps keep germs away and keeps your skin clean and healthy.

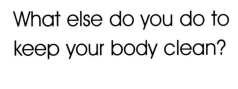

What else do you do to keep your body clean?

 TRY IT OUT!

Pick up different things and feel them. Do they feel rough or smooth? Are they warm or cold to touch? What else does your sense of touch tell you about them?

Under the Skin

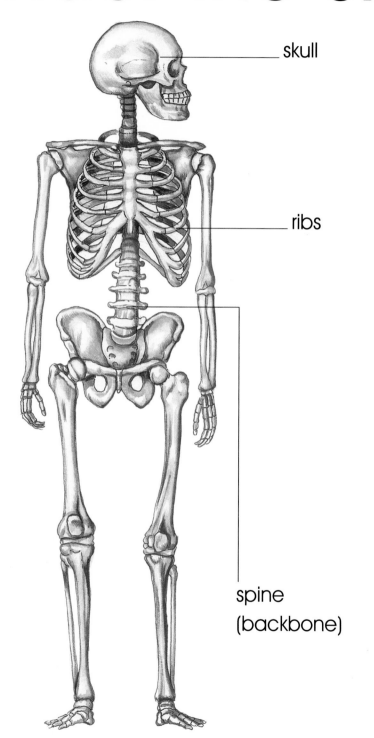

skull

ribs

spine
(backbone)

Can you feel the strong, hard **bones** under your skin? Bones give your body its shape.

You have 206 bones joined together by **joints**. Joints let you bend and move.

TRY IT OUT!

Your knees are joints. Bend them. Can you feel how they move backward and forward like hinges on a door?

Your shoulders are joints, too. Move your arm. Can you make it go round and round?

What other joints can you find?

Your bones and skin protect the parts of your body you cannot see. These are the parts of you that make your body work day and night.

These are just some of the parts inside your body. Each one has a special job to do.

Ribs are like a cage protecting your **heart** and **lungs**. Can you feel your rib bones on your chest?

Tap your head. Can you feel your hard **skull**? Your skull protects your brain.

👁️ LOOK AGAIN

Look again at page 11 to find out why your brain is important.

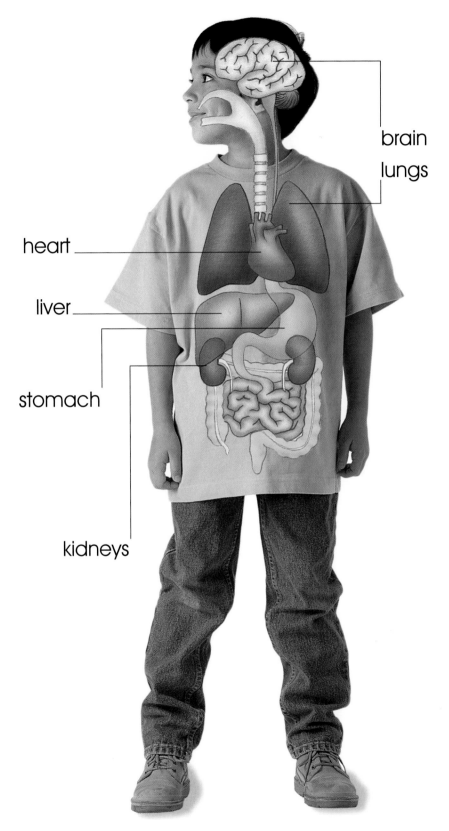

brain

lungs

heart

liver

stomach

kidneys

19

Breathing

Look at all the different things the people in these pictures are doing. They are all breathing air in and out of their lungs, even the boy who is asleep. Your body needs **oxygen** from the air all the time—that's why you can't hold your breath for very long.

💡 **THINK ABOUT IT!**

Why is it difficult to stay under water for very long when you go swimming?

You breathe fresh air in through your nose and mouth. Breathe in and feel your chest getting bigger as your lungs fill with air.

You breathe stale air out through your nose and mouth, too. Breathe out. Can you feel your body pushing out the stale air?

 **TRY IT OUT!**

Dangle a tissue in front of your face. Breathe deeply and watch the tissue move away from you as you breathe out and then toward you as you breathe in.

21

Pumping Blood

Look at the inside of your wrists. Can you see some blue colored tubes under the skin? Those are **blood vessels**. They carry **blood** all around your body.

Your blood does a very important job. It collects oxygen from your lungs and takes it to every part of your body. It also carries around your body all the goodness and energy from the food you eat.

Have you ever cut yourself and seen your own red blood?
Blood helps your cut heal.

You should wash your cut to help keep out the germs.

Your blood will dry into a scab that covers the cut, while your skin heals underneath.

Put your hand on your chest. Can you feel your heart beat? Your heart is doing its job. It pumps your blood to every part of your body.

Your heart never stops working, day or night, so your blood never stops moving all around your body.

When you are exercising, you need more energy from your blood, so your heart works harder.

 TRY IT OUT!

Feel your heart beat when you are sitting or standing still. Now run, jump, or skip for a minute or two. Feel you heart again. What do you notice?

23

On the Move

Did you know that every time you move, you use your **muscles**?
You use muscles to move your arms and legs. You use muscles to bite and chew. You even use muscles when you smile or blink.

Muscles are attached to your bones by strong cords called **tendons**. You can feel a big tendon, called the Achilles tendon, in the back of your ankle, just above your heel.

You have big, strong muscles attached to the bones in your legs. These muscles pull the bones in your leg when you bend, walk, or run.

 TRY IT OUT!

Bend your knees up and down. Feel what happens to the muscles above your knees and in the back of your legs as you move.

Exercise makes your muscles work hard and keeps them strong and healthy.

Did you know that your heart is a muscle? It works all the time. The muscles that let you breathe are always working, too.

 **LOOK AGAIN**

Look again at page 23. What happens to your heart when you exercise?

Sleep Well

Your heart never stops beating, you never stop breathing, and your brain never stops working. But sometimes, your body needs to rest.

You need plenty of sleep to stay healthy.

As you sleep through the night, your body doesn't have to work so hard. You breathe more slowly and your heart beats less quickly.

When you are asleep, your brain gets a rest from thinking and working out problems—although some of the time you are dreaming.

Your muscles get a rest from moving about.

Sleep gives your body time to get better when you are ill.

After a good night's sleep, you wake up ready for another busy day.

Sleep is a good time for growing, too. How many hours' sleep do you usually have at night? Ask an adult how many hours' sleep they usually have. Who has the most sleep?

 THINK ABOUT IT!

Why do babies need so much sleep?

27

Useful Words

Blood Blood is the red liquid that carries oxygen from your lungs and goodness from your food to every part of your body.

Blood vessels Your blood travels all around your body through tubes called blood vessels.

Bones Bones are strong and hard. They make a frame called a skeleton to support your body.

Brain You think with your brain and make sense of the world around you.

Disease A disease makes you feel ill. Sometimes an injection can protect you from catching a disease.

Energy People use energy from food to keep warm, to grow, and to move.

Germs Germs carry diseases that can make you feel ill. Germs are too tiny to see.

Heart Your heart is a strong muscle that pumps blood all around your body. It works all the time.

Joints Joints are the places where your bones are joined together. They let your body bend and move. Knees and elbows are joints.

Lungs You have two lungs that are like bags inside your chest. They fill up with air when you breathe in and empty when you breathe out.

Melanin Melanin is a dark color in your skin. It helps protect you from sunburn.

Muscles Muscles are attached to your bones so that you can move them. Other muscles help you breathe and swallow food. Your heart is a muscle that pumps blood.

Nerves Nerves connect your brain to the rest of your body. They take messages to and from your brain about what you sense and do.

Oxygen Oxygen is a kind of gas that is part of the air we breathe. Our bodies need oxygen to work.

Ribs Your ribs are the bones that make a cage that protects your heart and lungs.

Saliva Saliva is a liquid that is made in your mouth. It helps your food to slip down when you swallow it.

Senses Seeing, hearing, feeling, smelling, and tasting are the five senses. You use your senses to tell what is going on all around you.

Skull Your skull is the bone in your head that protects your brain and gives your head its shape.

Stomach When you eat, your food goes into your stomach, where juices break food down into very tiny pieces.

Tendons Tendons are strong cords that attach your muscles to your bones.

Index

About This Book

Children are natural scientists. They learn by touching and feeling, noticing, asking questions and trying things out for themselves. The books in the *It's Science!* series are designed for the way children learn. Familiar objects are used as starting points for further learning. *You and Your Body* starts by naming parts of the body and explores how the body works.

Each double page spread introduces a new topic, such as breathing. Information is given, questions asked and activities suggested that encourage children to make discoveries and develop new ideas for themselves. Look out for these panels throughout the book:

TRY IT OUT! indicates a simple activity, using safe materials, that proves or explores a point.
THINK ABOUT IT! indicates a question inspired by the information on the page but which points the reader to areas not covered by the book.
LOOK AGAIN introduces a cross-referencing activity which links themes and facts through the book.

Encourage children not to take the familiar world for granted. Point things out, ask questions and enjoy making scientific discoveries together.